THIS
BOOK OF QVESTIONS
BELONGS TO

_____

LISTEN TO YOUR HEART. IT WILL GIVE YOU ANSWERS.

ESCUCHA LA VOZ QUE LLEVAS DENTRO DE TI, tE DARA LAS RESPUESTAS.

DATE

FECHA

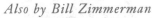

Also by Bill Zimmerman

How to Tape Instant Oral Biographies
Make Beliefs: A Gift for Your Imagination
LifeLines: A Book of Hope
The Little Book of Joy
Dogmas: Simple Truths from a Wise Pet
Make Beliefs for Kids
A Book of Sunshine

A BOOK OF QUESTIONS

A PLAYFUL JOURNAL TO KEEP THOUGHTS & FEELINGS

Questions in English and Spanish
PREGUNTAS EN INGLES Y ESPAÑOL

BILL ZIMMERMAN

ILLUSTRATIONS BY TOM BLOOM

SCHOLASTIC INC.
New York Toronto
London Auckland Sydney

For Carlota, who has so many questions:
May you find the answers,
and never take "no" for an answer.

ISBN 0-590-00672-X

Copyright © 1984, 1993, 1997 by William Zimmerman.
Drawings copyright © 1997 by Tom Bloom.
Cover design by FineLine Marketing and Design.
Cover illustrations by Tom Bloom.
Translations by Teodorina Bello de Zimmerman.

All rights reserved. Published by Scholastic Inc., 555 Broadway, New York,
NY 10012, by arrangement with Sourcebooks.

SCHOLASTIC and associated logos are trademarks and/or registered
trademarks of Scholastic Inc.

12 11 10 9 8 7 6 5 4 3 2 1   8 9/9 0 1 2 3/0

Printed in the U.S.A.   08
First Scholastic printing, February 1998

FOREWORD

This little book will be unlike any other you have read because it will be written by you. It will hold the thoughts and feelings that belong only to you.

So many of us say we want to keep a journal, but when we decide to try, we're not quite sure what to write in it.

This book will enable you to begin, because it provides a simple way for you to think about your life: it questions you and encourages you to respond with written thoughts.

And such writing will help you decipher yourself.

The questions in this book are here to help you talk to and know yourself better through your written responses to them. They are questions I have asked myself throughout my life. I believe they will have meaning for you, too.

They are here to help you take your pulse, to hear your special voice.

The book was made small, to be carried on your person like some bible that contains the clearest moments of your life when you took the time to write to yourself.

Its questions are meant to free you, to amuse you, to puzzle you, to help you break away from the hard work you do.

Choose the ones you want to answer in any order: feel free to change them to meet your own needs— they are merely a guide. Simply write whatever thoughts come to mind in the space provided under the question, and add to them with time. There also is a place to write the date for the thought, or pensamiento.

Don't worry if you don't have answers to a particular question. Come back to it when you feel ready. There are blank pages in the back to add your own questions. And, when you run out of space, begin another journal.

Write in this book only when you want to. You may even want to draw your answers or write your thoughts in your own secret language.

This little book is yours to define yourself; but it can be shared with those whom you want to know more about you.

Enjoy my book of questions. Through use, it becomes your book of answers. Remember, once you complete it, there will be no other book like it in the world. It is created by you. Start this book when you are ready to listen to yourself.

Bill Zimmerman

P.S. Dear Reader,

For this new edition, I have added more than a dozen new questions, provided space for you to doodle or draw your responses, and included a special message written in sign language than can be deciphered with help from the sign language alphabet found on page 8. By spelling out the sign letters found on the bottom of each right-hand page, you will discover this message to sweeten your path to answers. I use sign language in this book because, increasingly, many of us are learning this beautiful language as a way to communicate with others. It is a quiet language and goes well with the intent of this book, to help you hear what is within you. You will also see that the book's questions are written in Spanish, as so many of us are beginning to use this language in our daily lives.

P.P.S.

AND REMEMBER, THERE ARE NO
»RIGHT« ANSWERS ... ONLY THOSE
THAT COME FROM YOUR HEART.

SIGN ON....

AMERICAN SIGN LANGUAGE ALPHABET

As You Turn The Pages, You Will Find The Signs For Different Letters On The Bottom Of Each Right-Hand Page. Decipher Them In Order And You Will Discover That They Spell Out An Encouraging Message To Help You On Your Path To Answers.

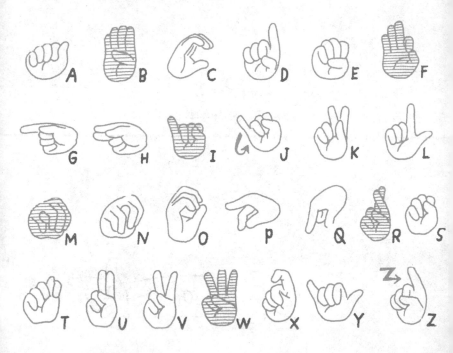

How To Use This Journal

I originally wrote this book of questions as a way to help me think through the many questions I had in my life, for posing questions puts one on the path to finding answers.

I found that the book, once published, took on its own life. Over the years I've received letters from a wide range of users— from teachers and children in elementary schools, to teenagers and young adults looking for fun and self-enlightenment, to harried business executives and working parents seeking a way to relax and touch base with themselves, to people in senior citizen centers wanting to reflect on their lives.

Many educators use this book of questions to encourage youngsters and adults who are learning how to read and write English to practice language, reading, and creative skills. Many teachers use the individual questions as subjects for essays, poems, and plays. Some have even replicated in poster form individual pages and asked each student to enter his or her contribution. Others have used the book as a model to encourage students to write their own questions and answers. That is what I hope will happen—that this book will prod you to articulate the questions in your heart and that you will not be afraid to look yourself in the eye.

This book has also been used by many counselors in therapy and recovery programs that encourage journal-keeping as a way to help people heal. I have found that writing a few minutes a day in this little book is in many ways a form of praying and a helpmate in coming to better self-understanding.

For those who teach young and old how to read and write English or Spanish as a second language, A Book of Questions can be an invaluable tool for helping people try their new language skills in a nonthreatening manner. The questions are also in Spanish.

In the home and workplace, where pressure seems to increase as we juggle our many responsibilities, taking a few minutes out of the day to write down what we think and feel can provide a welcome respite for workers, homemakers, and caretakers. It is a way of saying to oneself, "I'm going to do something special for me today, if only for a few minutes."

For those of you who are parents, grandparents, aunts and uncles, or big brothers and sisters, why not sit down with the children in your life one night or Sunday morning and answer a question together? Doing so can give you a unique insight into how your minds and spirits work. If your children are too young to read the questions on the page, you can read them aloud and ask the children to dictate a response that you can write for them. This will reinforce the value of their voice. That often was the way I encouraged my own daughter to write and to believe that what she thought was important.

But there is one thing to remember, too, in using this book. It is foremost a resource to have fun with, the fun that comes from having your own private journal to keep the thoughts that are yours alone, that capture your jokes and laughter, your sweet madness, your special way of looking at life and the world. There are even special pages on which you can draw your responses, and there is space, too, for your doodles. Make this book your own personal treasure chest.

A BOOK OF

QUESTIONS

A PLAYFUL JOURNAL TO KEEP THOUGHTS & FEELINGS

A Book of Questions

WHAT HAVE BEEN THE HAPPIEST TIMES OF YOUR LIFE?
¿CUALES HAN SIDO LAS EPOCAS MAS FELICES DE TU VIDA?

TUS PENSAMIENTOS / YOUR THOUGHTS

THIS LETTER IS

DATE / FECHA

A Book of Questions

DO A DOODLE ORTWOODLE

WHAT SPECIAL THING HAPPENED TO YOU TODAY?

¿QUE COSA ESPECIAL TE OCURRIO HOY?

—— TUS PENSAMIENTOS / YOUR THOUGHTS ——

DATE / FECHA

A Book of Questions

WHAT'S FUNNY ABOUT YOURSELF THAT
MAKES YOU SMILE WHEN YOU THINK
ABOUT IT?

¿HAY ALGO GRACIOSO EN TI QUE TE HAGA
SONREIR AL PENSAR EN ELLO?

TUS PENSAMIENTOS / YOUR THOUGHTS

DATE/FECHA

THIS
LETTER
IS

A Book of Questions

IF YOU HAD THREE MAGIC WISHES THAT COULD COME TRUE, WHAT WOULD THEY BE?
< YOU DON'T HAVE TO WRITE THEM ALL AT ONCE >
SI PUDIERAS REALIZAR TRES DESEOS MAGICOS... ¿CUALES SERIAN?
< NO TIENES QUE ESCRIBIRLOS TODOS A LA VEZ >

TUS PENSAMIENTOS / YOUR THOUGHTS

LET'S FACE IT

DATE / FECHA

A Book of Questions

WHAT
ARE YOUR
STRENGTHS
THAT GET YOU
THROUGH THE HARD TIMES?
¿QUE ES LO QUE TE DA FUERZAS PARA
SALIR ADELANTE EN LOS MOMENTOS DIFICILES?

—— TUS PENSAMIENTOS / YOUR THOUGHTS ——

DATE / FECHA

THIS
LETTER
IS

A Book of Questions

FACE VALUE

WHAT'S YOUR FAVORITE STORY?
¿CUAL ES TU CUENTO FAVORITO?

TUS PENSAMIENTOS/YOUR THOUGHTS

DATE/FECHA

A Book of Questions

IF THERE WERE NO TOMORROW,
WHAT WOULD YOU DO TODAY?
SI YA NO HUBIERA UN MAÑANA, ¿QUE HARIAS HOY?

——— TUS PENSAMIENTOS/YOUR THOUGHTS ———

DATE/FECHA

THIS
LETTER
IS

A Book of Questions

WHAT IS THE MOST IMPORTANT PIECE OF INFORMATION YOU'VE PICKED UP IN LIFE SO FAR?

¿CUAL ES LA INFORMACION MAS IMPORTANTE QUE TE HA DADO LA VIDA HASTA EL DIA DE HOY?

TUS PENSAMIENTOS

DRAWING ROOM

DATE

A Book of Questions

IF YOU COULD CREATE SOMETHING VERY BEAUTIFUL
FOR THE WORLD, WHAT WOULD IT BE?

SI PUDIERAS CREAR ALGO MUY BELLO PARA EL MUNDO "¿QUE SERIA?

——————— YOUR THOUGHTS ———————

_____

_____

_____

_____

_____

_____

F E C H A

IF YOU COULD DISCOVER A NEW STAR, WHAT WOULD YOU CALL IT?

SI PUDIERAS DESCUBRIR UNA ESTRELLA NUEVA "¿QUE NOMBRE LE DARIAS?

——————— YOUR THOUGHTS ———————

_____

_____

_____

_____

_____

F E C H A

THIS
LETTER
IS

A Book of Questions

DOODLE ALL YOU WANT

WHAT MAKES YOU MOST HAPPY?
¿QUÉ ES LO QUE TE HACE MÁS FELIZ?

———— TUS PENSAMIENTOS ————

D A T E

WHAT IS THE SMELL THAT MAKES YOU FEEL SAFE AND CARED FOR?
¿CUÁL ES EL OLOR QUE TE HACE SENTIR QUE TE CUIDAN Y TE QUIEREN?

———— TUS PENSAMIENTOS ————

D A T E

A Book of Questions

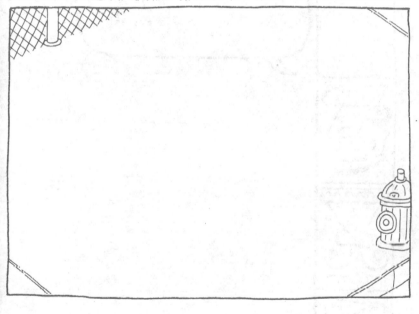

YOUR THOUGHTS

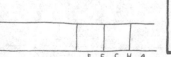

FECHA

THIS
LETTER
IS

A Book of Questions

DRAW YOUR OWN CONCLUSION

WHAT NEW THINGS WOULD YOU LIKE TO DO?

¿QUE COSAS NUEVAS TE GUSTARIA HACER?

———— TUS PENSAMIENTOS ————

D A T E

A Book of Questions

WHAT BAD MEMORY OR DREAM KEEPS PLAYING OVER
AND OVER IN YOUR HEAD LIKE A BROKEN MELODY?
¿QUE MAL RECUERDO O PESADILLA SE REPITE EN TU MENTE COMO
UNA MELODIA INTERMINABLE?

YOUR THOUGHTS

FECHA

THIS
LETTER
IS

A Book of Questions

FACE THE DAY

WHAT DID YOU LEARN TODAY?
¿QUE APRENDISTE HOY?

——— TUS PENSAMIENTOS ———

DATE

A Book of Questions

WHAT IS THE GREATEST EXPERIENCE YOU EVER HAD ?
¿CUAL ES LA EXPERIENCIA MAS FABULOSA QUE HAS TENIDO ?

YOUR THOUGHTS

FECHA

THIS LETTER IS

A Book of Questions

FACE YOURSELF TODAY

WHEN IT COMES DOWN TO IT, WHAT DO YOU REALLY BELIEVE IN?
A LA HORA DE LA VERDAD, ¿EN QUE CREES?

— TUS PENSAMIENTOS —

DATE

WHAT IS THE BEST FREE ADVICE YOU HAVE TO OFFER?
¿CUAL ES EL MEJOR CONSEJO QUE PUEDES OFRECER GRATIS?

— TUS PENSAMIENTOS —

DATE

A Book of Questions

WHAT KINDS OF PEOPLE DO YOU LIKE MOST?
¿QUE CLASE DE GENTE TE GUSTA MAS?

————— YOUR THOUGHTS —————

_____

_____

_____

_____

FECHA

IF YOU COULD GIVE A BEAT OF YOUR LIFE TO SOMEONE,
WHOM WOULD IT BE?
¿SI PUDIERAS DARLE A ALGUIEN UN LATIDO DE TU VIDA, A QUIEN SE LO DARIAS?

————— YOUR THOUGHTS —————

_____

_____

_____

_____

_____

THIS
LETTER
IS

FECHA

A Book of Questions

WHAT DO YOU THINK ABOUT DEATH?
¿QUE PIENSAS DE LA MUERTE?

TUS PENSAMIENTOS

DATE

WHAT WOULD YOU BE REBORN AS?
¿QUE SERIAS SI VOLVIERAS A NACER?

TUS PENSAMIENTOS

DATE

DOODLE DOODLE DO

A Book of Questions

YOU ARE A SORCERER AND HAVE THE POWER TO CAST A
SPELL. WHAT WORDS WOULD YOU USE, AND HOW WOULD
YOU USE THE SPELL?

ERES UN HECHICERO Y TIENES EL PODER DE ENCANTAR. ¿QUE PALABRAS
DIRIAS Y PARA QUE USARIAS EL HECHIZO?

———— YOUR THOUGHTS ————

F E C H A

IF YOU COULD WRITE A SWEET BLESSING,
WHAT WOULD YOU SAY?

SI PUDIERAS ESCRIBIR UNA BENDICION ··· ¿QUE DIRIAS?

———— YOUR THOUGHTS ————

F E C H A

THIS
LETTER
IS

A Book of Questions

WHAT WOULD YOU CHANGE ABOUT YOUR PARENTS IF YOU HAD THE POWER?

¿QUE COSA CAMBIARIAS EN TUS PADRES SI PUDIERAS HACERLO?

—— TUS PENSAMIENTOS ——

FACE FACTS

DATE

A Book of Questions

ONCE WHEN YOU WERE ILL AND YOU SAID YOU WOULD CHANGE IF ONLY YOU GOT WELL AGAIN, WHAT DID YOU MEAN?

UNA VEZ ESTUVISTE ENFERMO Y DIJISTE QUE IBAS A CAMBIAR TU MANERA DE SER SI TE ALIVIABAS. ¿QUE QUISISTE DECIR CON ESO?

——————— YOUR THOUGHTS ———————

FECHA

THIS LETTER IS

A Book of Questions

DRAW ON YOUR MEMORY

WHAT IS YOUR FAVORITE CHARACTER YOU HAVE READ ABOUT IN A BOOK OR SEEN IN A PLAY, AND WHAT MAKES THEM SO SPECIAL TO YOU? HOW ARE YOU LIKE OR DIFFERENT FROM THEM?

¿QUIEN ES ESE PERSONAJE FAVORITO TUYO DEL CUAL LEISTE EN UN LIBRO O A QUIEN VISTE EN UNA PELICULA? ¿POR QUE ES TAN ESPECIAL? ¿EN QUE TE PARECES O ERES DIFERENTE?

— TUS PENSAMIENTOS —

DATE

A Book of Questions

>> THE SAGE PAGE <<
WRITE, DRAW, OR COLOR THIS SPACE

YOUR THOUGHTS

THIS LETTER IS

F E C H A

A Book of Questions

FACE FORWARD

WHAT IS THE BEST THING THAT COULD EVER HAPPEN TO YOU?
¿QUE ES LO MEJOR QUE PODRIA OCURRIRTE?

——— TUS PENSAMIENTOS ———

DATE

IF YOU COULD TASTE A CLOUD, WHAT DO YOU THINK IT WOULD BE LIKE?
SI PUDIERAS PROBAR UNA NUBE, ¿QUE SABOR CREES QUE TENDRIA?

——— TUS PENSAMIENTOS ———

DATE

A Book of Questions

WHAT ARE THE THINGS YOU CAN DO TO ENJOY YOUR LIFE MORE?

¿QUE COSAS QUE PUEDES HACER PARA GOZAR MAS DE LA VIDA?

YOUR THOUGHTS

THIS LETTER IS

FECHA

A Book of Questions

DO A DOODLE ORTWOODLE

IF YOU COULD MAKE A GREAT MOVIE
OR WRITE A BOOK, WHAT WOULD IT BE ABOUT?
SI PUDIERAS FILMAR UNA GRAN PELICULA O
ESCRIBIR UN LIBRO" ¿DE QUE TRATARIA?

———— TUS PENSAMIENTOS ————

D A T E

WHAT IS THE SONG WITHIN YOU THAT
YEARNS TO COME OUT?
¿CUAL ES LA CANCION QUE LLEVAS POR DENTRO
QUE BUSCA SALIDA?

———— TUS PENSAMIENTOS ————

D A T E

A Book of Questions

WHAT MAKES YOU SO ANGRY OR HATEFUL ?

¿QUE ES LO QUE TE ENOJA MAS O LO QUE MAS DETESTAS?

YOUR THOUGHTS

THIS
LETTER
IS

FECHA

A Book of Questions

> ## WHAT ARE THE THINGS YOU CAN DO TO BE LESS LONELY?
> ### ¿QUE PUEDES HACER PARA NO SENTIRTE TAN SOLO?

———— TUS PENSAMIENTOS ————

DATE

A Book of Questions

WHAT IS YOUR MOST VALUABLE TREASURE? WHY IS IT SO?

¿CUAL ES TU TESORO MAS VALIOSO? ¿POR QUE?

— YOUR THOUGHTS —

FECHA

THIS LETTER IS

A Book of Questions

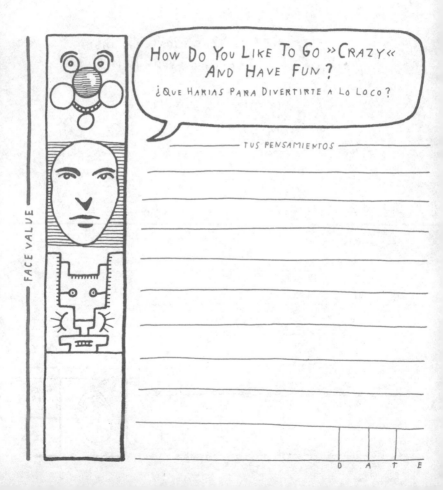

FACE VALUE

HOW DO YOU LIKE TO GO »CRAZY«
AND HAVE FUN?

¿QUE HARIAS PARA DIVERTIRTE A LO LOCO?

———————— TUS PENSAMIENTOS ————————

D A T E

A Book of Questions

WHAT ARE YOU MOST AFRAID OF ABOUT GROWING UP?

¿QUE ES LO QUE TE DA MAS MIEDO CUANDO PIENSAS EN QUE CADA DIA ERES MAYOR?

— YOUR THOUGHTS —

THIS LETTER IS

FECHA

A Book of Questions

DRAWING ROOM

$OMEONE HA$ GIVEN YOU A MILLION DOLLAR$. WHAT WOULD YOU DO WITH IT?

$I ALGUIEN TE DIERA UN MILLON DE DOLARE$" ¿QUE HARIA$ CON E$E DINERO?

TUS PENSAMIENTOS

DATE

A Book of Questions

WHAT NEW
LAND OR PLACE WOULD YOU LIKE TO GO TO?
¿A QUE NUEVO PAIS O LUGAR TE GUSTARIA IR?

————— YOUR THOUGHTS —————

THIS
LETTER
IS

FECHA

A Book of Questions

DOODLE ALL YOU WANT

WERE YOU EVER LOST? WHAT HAPPENED?
¿ALGUNA VEZ TE HAS PERDIDO? ¿QUE PASO?

———— TUS PENSAMIENTOS ————

D A T E

A Book of Questions

IF YOU COULD USE YOUR IMAGINATION
TO GET BACK AT SOMEONE
WHO HURT YOU, WHAT WOULD YOU DO TO THEM ?

SI PUDIERAS USAR TU IMAGINACION PARA DESQUITARTE
DE ALGUIEN QUE TE HIZO DAÑO ¿QUE HARIAS?

———————————— YOUR THOUGHTS ————————————

THIS
LETTER
IS

F E C H A

A Book of Questions

WHAT NEW THING DID YOU NOTICE TODAY?
¿EN QUE COSA NUEVA TE FIJASTE HOY?

TUS PENSAMIENTOS

DRAW YOUR OWN CONCLUSION

DATE

A Book of Questions

IF YOU COULD BE A FLOWER,
WHICH WOULD YOU BE? (DRAW IT.)
SI PUDIERAS SER UNA FLOR–
¿CUAL SERIAS? (DIBUJALA.)
—— YOUR THOUGHTS ——

IF YOU COULD BE A COLOR,
WHAT WOULD YOU BE?
(PUT IT ON THIS PAGE TO SEE)

SI PUDIERAS SER UN COLOR–
¿CUAL SERIAS?

(COLOREA EN ESTA HOJA PARA VERLO.)
—— YOUR THOUGHTS ——

THIS
LETTER
IS

FECHA

A Book of Questions

WHAT IS YOUR SADDEST MEMORY?
¿CUAL ES EL RECUERDO MAS TRISTE QUE TIENES?

TUS PENSAMIENTOS

FACE THE DAY

D   A   T   E

A Book of Questions

>> A MESSAGE TO THE MASSES <<
WRITE · DRAW OR COLOR THIS SPACE

YOUR THOUGHTS

THIS LETTER IS

FECHA

A Book of Questions

WHAT IS THE HARDEST RIDDLE YOU KNOW?
¿CUAL ES LA ADIVINANZA MAS DIFICIL QUE CONOCES?

———— TUS PENSAMIENTOS ————

FACE YOURSELF TODAY

D A T E

A Book of Questions

HAVE YOU EVER FRIGHTENED SOMEONE OR HURT THEM? WHAT DID YOU DO TO THEM? WHY?

¿TU ALGUNA VEZ ASUSTASTE A ALGUIEN U LE HICISTE DAÑO? ¿QUE LE HICISTE? ¿POR QUE?

──── YOUR THOUGHTS ────

FECHA

THIS LETTER IS

A Book of Questions

DOODLE DOODLE DO

WHAT ARE THE THINGS YOU DON'T LIKE IN OTHER PEOPLE?

¿QUE COSAS NO TE GUSTAN DE OTRA GENTE?

——— TUS PENSAMIENTOS ———

DATE

A Book of Questions

IF YOU COULD BE A TOY,
WHAT WOULD YOU BE?

SI PUDIERAS CONVERTIRTE EN
JUGUETE ... ¿QUE SERIAS?

———— YOUR THOUGHTS ————

FECHA

THIS
LETTER
IS

A Book of Questions

FACE FACTS

IN ALL OF LANGUAGE, WHAT IS THE MOST BEAUTIFUL WORD YOU KNOW?

¿CUAL ES LA PALABRA MAS BELLA QUE CONOCES EN TODOS LOS IDIOMAS?

TUS PENSAMIENTOS

D A T E

WHAT ABOUT SOME WORD THAT DOES NOT YET EXIST?

¿CUAL ES ESA PALABRA QUE NO EXISTE TODAVIA?

TUS PENSAMIENTOS

D A T E

A Book of Questions

WHEN ARE THE TIMES YOU FEEL MOST LIKE HIDING? WHERE WOULD YOU LIKE TO GO?

¿EN QUE OCASIONES QUISIERAS ESCONDERTE? ¿A DONDE IRIAS?

—— YOUR THOUGHTS ——

FECHA

THIS LETTER IS

A Book of Questions

DRAW ON YOUR MEMORY

IF YOU WERE TO TELL THE TALE OF YOUR LIFE TO SOMEONE, IN A WAY NO ONE WOULD KNOW IT'S YOU, WHAT WOULD YOUR STORY BE?

SI FUERAS A CONTARLE A ALGUIEN LA HISTORIA DE TU VIDA DE MANERA QUE NO SE SUPIERA QUE ERES TU, ¿COMO LA CONTARIAS?

———— TUS PENSAMIENTOS ————

A Book of Questions

THIS
LETTER
IS

FECHA

A Book of Questions

IF YOU COULD CLIMB A STAIRWAY OF STARS, WHAT WOULD YOU HOPE TO FIND AT THE TOP?

SI PUDIERAS SUBIR UNA ESCALERA DE ESTRELLAS, ¿QUE ESPERARIAS ENCONTRAR EN LO ALTO?

TUS PENSAMIENTOS

FACE FORWARD

D A T E

A Book of Questions

HOW DID YOU LEARN TO STAND ON YOUR OWN TWO FEET?

¿CÓMO APRENDISTE A MANTENERTE EN PIE POR TI MISMO?

———— YOUR THOUGHTS ————

THIS LETTER IS

FECHA

A Book of Questions

WHAT IS THE WAY YOU LIKE LOVE TO BE SHOWN TO YOU? HOW DO YOU SHOW LOVE?
¿DE QUE MANERA TE GUSTA QUE TE MUESTREN AMOR?
¿COMO DEMUESTRAS AMOR?

TUS PENSAMIENTOS

DO A DOODLE OR TWOODLE

DATE

A Book of Questions

WHAT MAKES YOU CRY?
¿QUE TE HACE LLORAR?

YOUR THOUGHTS

FECHA

THIS LETTER IS

A Book of Questions

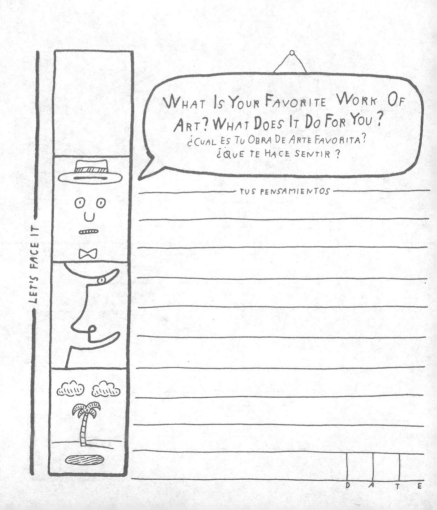

LET'S FACE IT

WHAT IS YOUR FAVORITE WORK OF ART? WHAT DOES IT DO FOR YOU?

¿CUAL ES TU OBRA DE ARTE FAVORITA? ¿QUE TE HACE SENTIR?

—— TUS PENSAMIENTOS ——

DATE

A Book of Questions

WHAT ARE SOME THINGS YOU WERE ONCE AFRAID OF, BUT ARE NO LONGER?

¿QUÉ COSAS TE HACÍAN SENTIR MIEDO ANTES, PERO AHORA NO?

— YOUR THOUGHTS —

_____

_____

_____

_____

FECHA

WHEN WAS THE TIME YOU FOUND THE POWER WITHIN YOU?

¿CUÁNDO ENCONTRASTE EL PODER QUE LLEVAS DENTRO DE TI?

— YOUR THOUGHTS —

_____

_____

_____

THIS LETTER IS

FECHA

FACE VALUE

IF YOU WERE GOING TO A MASKED BALL AND COULD FIND A COSTUME TO MATCH YOUR WILDEST DREAMS, HOW WOULD YOU LOOK? DESCRIBE IT OR DRAW IT SO YOU WON'T FORGET.

SI FUERAS A IR A UN BAILE DE MASCARAS Y ENCONTRARAS UN DISFRAZ QUE REFLEJARA TUS SUEÑOS MAS DESCABELLADOS, ¿CUAL SERIA? DESCRIBELO O DIBUJALO PARA QUE NO LO OLVIDES.

—— TUS PENSAMIENTOS ——

DATE

A Book of Questions

WHAT BIG PROBLEMS ARE YOU STRUGGLING WITH? WHAT BIG PROBLEMS DID YOU HAVE A YEAR AGO? HOW DID YOU SOLVE THEM?

¿CON QUE PROBLEMAS GRANDES LUCHAS? ¿QUE PROBLEMAS GRANDES TENIAS HACE UN AÑO, Y COMO LOS RESOLVISTE?

—— YOUR THOUGHTS ——

THIS
LETTER
IS

FECHA

A Book of Questions

DRAWING ROOM

WHAT KIND OF INVENTION WOULD YOU LIKE TO INVENT? WHAT WOULD IT BE?

¿QUÉ CLASE DE INVENTO TE GUSTARÍA CREAR? ¿QUÉ SERÍA?

————— TUS PENSAMIENTOS —————

DATE

A Book of Questions

WHEN ARE THE TIMES
YOU FEEL MOST

LOST
&
LONELY?

¿EN QUE MOMENTOS TE SIENTES
MAS PERDIDO Y SOLO?

—————— YOUR THOUGHTS ——————

THIS
LETTER
IS

FECHA

A Book of Questions

WHAT KIND OF PERSON DO YOU WANT TO BE? HOW, IF AT ALL, WOULD YOU CHANGE?

¿QUE CLASE DE PERSONA QUIERES SER? ¿DE QUE MANERA CAMBIARIAS SI FUESE NECESARIO?

DOODLE ALL YOU WANT

TUS PENSAMIENTOS

DATE

A Book of Questions

HAT ARE THE (THINGS) YOU WANT
TO TELL A CHILD TO HELP
THEM ALONG IN LIFE ?

¿QUE COSAS QUISIERAS CONTARLE A UN NIÑO
PARA QUE LE FUERA BIEN EN LA VIDA ?

————— YOUR THOUGHTS —————

THIS
LETTER
IS

FECHA

A Book of Questions

WHAT NEW DISCOVERY
DO YOU WANT TO MAKE?
¿QUÉ DESCUBRIMIENTO
NUEVO QUIERES HACER?

DRAW YOUR OWN CONCLUSION

—— TUS PENSAMIENTOS ——

D A T E

A Book of Questions

>> SPARKS IN THE DARK <<
WRITE · DRAW OR COLOR THIS SPACE

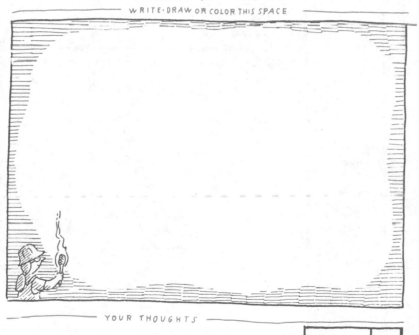

YOUR THOUGHTS

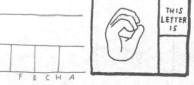

THIS LETTER IS

FECHA

A Book of Questions

FACE THE DAY

WHOM DO YOU ADMIRE? WHY?
¿A QUIEN ADMIRAS? ¿POR QUE?

————— TUS PENSAMIENTOS —————

DATE

A Book of Questions

WHAT BITTERNESS DO YOU HAVE
IN YOUR SOUL?
¿QUE AMARGURA LLEVAS EN EL ALMA?

———— YOUR THOUGHTS ————

THIS
LETTER
IS

FECHA

A Book of Questions

FACE YOURSELF TODAY

TELL ME A GREAT JOKE,
¡CUENTAME UN BUEN CHISTE!

—— TUS PENSAMIENTOS ——

D A T E

A Book of Questions

WHAT ARE THE THINGS THAT MAKE YOU FEEL MORE POWERFUL
IN LIFE? WHAT WOULD YOU DO WITH MORE POWER?

¿QUE COSAS TE HACEN SENTIR MAS PODEROSO EN LA VIDA?
¿QUE HARIAS SI TUVIERAS MAS PODER?

———— YOUR THOUGHTS ————

THIS
LETTER
IS

FECHA

A Book of Questions

DOODLE DOODLE DO

WHAT HAS BEEN THE HARDEST THING
YOU HAVE HAD TO DO SO FAR IN YOUR LIFE?
AND HOW DID YOU DO IT?

¿QUE ES LO MAS DIFICIL QUE HAS TENIDO QUE
HACER EN LA VIDA? ¿COMO LO HICISTE?

—— TUS PENSAMIENTOS ——

DATE

A Book of Questions

WHAT IS THE QUESTION ? YOU'RE AFRAID
TO ASK YOURSELF?

¿CUAL ES LA PREGUNTA QUE TE DA MAS TEMOR HACERTE A TI MISMO?

—————————— YOUR THOUGHTS ——————————

THIS
LETTER
IS

FECHA

A Book of Questions

FACE FACTS

WHAT'S THE FUNNIEST THING THAT EVER HAPPENED TO YOU?

¿QUE ES LA COSA MAS DIVERTIDA QUE TE HAYA OCURRIDO?

TUS PENSAMIENTOS

DATE

A Book of Questions

A Book of Questions

DRAW ON YOUR MEMORY

WHAT WAS THE MOST DIFFICULT
TIME YOU HAD TO GET OVER?

¿CUAL HA SIDO EL MOMENTO MAS DIFICIL
QUE HAS VIVIDO?

— TUS PENSAMIENTOS —

D A T E

A Book of Questions

COULD YOU WRITE ←SOMETHING IN A
SECRET LANGUAGE THAT NO ONE ELSE COULD
FIGURE OUT? (PLEASE WRITE THE TRANSLATION

NMOD EDISAN SOME PLACE ON THIS PAGE JUST IN
CASE YOU FORGET WHAT THE WORDS OR SOUNDS MEAN.)

¿PODRIAS ESCRIBIR ALGO EN UN IDIOMA SECRETO QUE NADIE
MAS PUEDE DESCIFRAR? (POR FAVOR ESCRIBE LA TRADUCCION SEVER TA
EN ESTA PAGINA POR SI ACASO OLVIDAS EL SIGNIFICADO DE LAS PALABRAS
O LOS SONIDOS.)

───── YOUR THOUGHTS ─────

THIS
LETTER
IS

FECHA

A Book of Questions

FACE FORWARD

WHAT'S GETTING IN YOUR WAY?
¿QUE OBSTACULOS TIENES?

—— TUS PENSAMIENTOS ——

D A T E

A Book of Questions

IF YOU COULD BE A SMELL,
WHAT WOULD YOU BE?

SI PUDIERAS SER UN OLOR... ¿CUAL SERIAS?

———— YOUR THOUGHTS ————

IF YOU COULD BE A MONSTER,
WHAT WOULD YOU BE LIKE?

SI PUDIERAS SER UN MONSTRUO... ¿COMO SERIAS?

———— YOUR THOUGHTS ————

THIS LETTER IS

FECHA

A Book of Questions

DO A DOODLE OR TWOODLE

WHAT ARE THE THINGS YOU LIKE ABOUT YOURSELF? WHAT'S GOOD ABOUT YOU?
¿QUE COSAS TE GUSTAN MAS DE TI?
¿QUE ES LO MEJOR QUE HAY EN TI?

——— TUS PENSAMIENTOS ———

DATE

A Book of Questions

WHAT DO YOU EXPECT
FROM DEATH?
¿QUE ESPERAS DE LA MUERTE?
——— YOUR THOUGHTS ———

FECHA

THIS
LETTER
IS

A Book of Questions

LET'S FACE IT

WHAT KIND OF HERO OR HEROINE WOULD YOU WANT TO BE?

¿QUE CLASE DE HEROE O HEROINA DESEARIAS SER?

———— TUS PENSAMIENTOS ————

D A T E

IF YOU WERE TO PERFORM AN ACT OF GRACE, WHAT WOULD YOU DO?

SI FUERAS A REALIZAR UN ACTO DE GRACIA "
¿QUE HARIAS?

———— TUS PENSAMIENTOS ————

D A T E

A Book of Questions

WHAT ARE SOME OF THE THINGS THAT STILL FRIGHTEN YOU? HOW CAN YOU FIGHT BACK?

¿CUALES SON ALGUNAS DE LAS COSAS QUE AUN TE ASUSTAN? ¿DE QUE MANERA PUEDES DEFENDERTE?

———— YOUR THOUGHTS ————

THIS LETTER IS

FECHA

A Book of Questions

FACE VALUE

WHAT DO YOU HATE MOST ?
¿QUE ES LO QUE MAS ODIAS ?

——— TUS PENSAMIENTOS ———

D A T E

WHAT IS YOUR PERSONAL MOTTO ?
¿CUAL ES TU LEMA PERSONAL ?

——— TUS PENSAMIENTOS ———

D A T E

A Book of Questions

WHAT ARE SOME THINGS YOU HAVE ACHIEVED IN YOUR LIFE SO FAR?

¿QUE METAS HAS ALCANZADO EN TU VIDA HASTA HOY?

————— YOUR THOUGHTS —————

_____

_____

_____

_____

_____

_____

_____

_____

_____

_____

_____

FECHA

THIS LETTER IS

A Book of Questions

DRAWING ROOM

WHAT HAVE YOU LEARNED FROM
YOUR MISTAKES?
¿QUE HAS APRENDIDO DE LOS ERRORES
QUE HAS COMETIDO?

—— TUS PENSAMIENTOS ——

D A T E

A Book of Questions

IF YOU COULD STEP OUTSIDE YOUR BODY
TO SEE YOURSELF CLEARLY, WHAT KIND OF PERSON
WOULD YOU SEE 👁 ? HOW WOULD YOU LIKE TO BE ?

SI PUDIERAS SALIR DE TU CUERPO PARA VERTE
CLARAMENTE ... ¿QUE CLASE DE PERSONA VERIAS ?
¿COMO TE GUSTARIA SER ?

———————YOUR THOUGHTS———————

THIS
LETTER
IS

FECHA

A Book of Questions

DOODLE ALL YOU WANT

WHAT WAS THE SADDEST TIME
IN YOUR LIFE?

¿CUAL HA SIDO LA EPOCA MAS
TRISTE DE TU VIDA?

TUS PENSAMIENTOS

D A T E

A Book of Questions

WHAT NAME WOULD YOU CHOOSE IF YOU COULD
NAME YOURSELF? WHY THIS NAME? DOES
IT HAVE A MEANING?

¿QUE NOMBRE ESCOGERIAS PARA TI SI PUDIERAS? ¿POR QUE
ESE NOMBRE? ¿TIENE ALGUN SIGNIFICADO?

YOUR THOUGHTS

IF WE WERE TO BECOME RAINBOW PEOPLE, WHAT
COLOR WOULD YOU CHOOSE?

SI NOS FUERAMOS A CONVERTIR EN LA GENTE DEL ARCO IRIS,
¿QUE COLOR ESCOGERIAS?

YOUR THOUGHTS

FECHA

THIS
LETTER
IS

A Book of Questions

DRAW YOUR OWN CONCLUSION

WHAT CARES WOULD YOU WISH TO DROP?

¿QUE PREOCUPACIONES QUISIERAS DEJAR DE LADO?

——— TUS PENSAMIENTOS ———

DATE

A Book of Questions

>> WALL SCRAWL <<
WRITE · DRAW OR COLOR THIS SPACE

YOUR THOUGHTS

FECHA

THIS
LETTER
IS

A Book of Questions

FACE THE DAY

WHAT ARE THE THINGS ABOUT YOUR PARENTS OR SOMEONE CLOSE TO YOU THAT WORRY YOU?
¿QUE COSAS TE PREOCUPAN ACERCA DE TUS PADRES O DE ALGUIEN CERCANO A TI?

——— TUS PENSAMIENTOS ———

D A T E

A Book of Questions

IF YOU COULD BE DIFFERENT, HOW WOULD YOU BE?

Si Pudieras Ser Distinto, ¿Como Serias?

—————— YOUR THOUGHTS ——————

_____

_____

_____

_____

_____

_____

_____

_____

_____

_____

THIS
LETTER
IS

F E C H A

A Book of Questions

FACE YOURSELF TODAY

WHAT ARE THE THINGS YOU
WANT TO LEARN?
¿QUE COSAS QUIERES APRENDER?

TUS PENSAMIENTOS

DATE

A Book of Questions

WHAT MAKES
YOU SAD?
¿QUE TE
ENTRISTECE?

———— YOUR THOUGHTS ————

THIS
LETTER
IS

FECHA

A Book of Questions

DOODLE DOODLE DO

WHAT ARE YOUR HOPES IN LIFE?
¿CUALES SON LAS ILUSIONES DE TU VIDA?

— TUS PENSAMIENTOS —

DATE

A Book of Questions

HAT STRANGE ADVENTURE WOULD YOU LIKE TO HAVE?
¿QUÉ AVENTURA RARA TE GUSTARÍA TENER?

———————— YOUR THOUGHTS ————————

FECHA

THIS
LETTER
IS

A Book of Questions

FACE FACTS

WHAT IS THERE IN YOUR LIFE
THAT YOU TAKE PRIDE IN ?
¿QUE COSA TE ENORGULLECE DE TU VIDA?

_____
_____
_____
_____
_____
_____
_____
_____
_____
_____
_____
_____

DATE

A Book of Questions

WHAT IS YOUR FAVORITE DOODLE?

¿CUAL ES TU DIBUJITO FAVORITO?

— YOUR THOUGHTS —

FECHA

THIS LETTER IS

A Book of Questions

WHAT WILL BE THE NEXT MILESTONE IN YOUR LIFE?

¿CUAL SERA EL PROXIMO ACONTECIMIENTO IMPORTANTE DE TU VIDA?

TUS PENSAMIENTOS

DATE

A Book of Questions

HAT WAS THE MOST WONDERFUL
THING THAT EVER HAPPENED TO YOU?

¿CUAL HA SIDO LA COSA MAS MARAVILLOSA
QUE HAS VIVIDO?

— YOUR THOUGHTS —

THIS
LETTER
IS

FECHA

A Book of Questions

FACE FORWARD

WHO TOUCHED YOU TODAY?
¿QUIEN TE LLEGO AL ALMA HOY?

———— TUS PENSAMIENTOS ————

D A T E

REMEMBER A KINDNESS THAT
WAS SHOWN YOU?
¿TE ACUERDAS DE ALGUN ACTO BONDADOSO
QUE ALGUIEN TUVO CONTIGO?

———— TUS PENSAMIENTOS ————

D A T E

A Book of Questions

WHAT TRUTH HAVE YOU LEARNED THAT YOU WANT TO SHARE?

¿QUE VERDAD HAS APPRENDIDO QUE QUISIERAS COMPARTIR?

—— YOUR THOUGHTS ——

FECHA

THIS LETTER IS

A Book of Questions

DO A DOODLE OR TWOODLE

IF YOU COULD BE A SOUND, WHAT WOULD YOU BE?

SI PUDIERAS SER UN SONIDO" ¿CUAL SERIAS?

———— TUS PENSAMIENTOS ————

D A T E

IF YOU COULD BE A MUSICAL INSTRUMENT, WHICH WOULD YOU BE?

SI PUDIERAS SER UN INSTRUMENTO MUSICAL, ¿CUAL SERIAS?

———— TUS PENSAMIENTOS ————

D A T E

A Book of Questions

IF YOU COULD WRITE A POEM OR SING A SONG,
WHAT WOULD IT BE ? HOW WOULD IT GO ?
SI PUDIERAS ESCRIBIR UN POEMA O CANTAR UNA CANCION ~
¿CUAL SERIA? ¿CÓMO ES ?

YOUR THOUGHTS

FECHA

THIS LETTER IS

A Book of Questions

WHAT CAN YOU TEACH OTHERS ?

¿QUE LES PUEDES ENSEÑAR A OTROS?

———— TUS PENSAMIENTOS ————

LET'S FACE IT

DATE

WHAT FUNNY OR PUZZLING STORY HAVE YOU HEARD LATELY?

¿QUÉ COSA CHISTOSA O DESCONCERTANTE HAS OÍDO RECIENTEMENTE?

YOUR THOUGHTS

FECHA

THIS LETTER IS

A Book of Questions

FACE VALUE

WHAT SURPRISES YOU?
¿QUE TE SORPRENDE?

———TUS PENSAMIENTOS———

DATE

A Book of Questions

HOW COULD YOU TREAT YOURSELF BETTER?

¿QUE TENDRIAS QUE HACER PARA TRATARTE MEJOR?

———— YOUR THOUGHTS ————

FECHA

THIS LETTER IS

A Book of Questions

DRAWING ROOM

WHOM DO YOU LOVE ? WHY ?

¿A QUIEN AMAS? ¿POR QUE ?

—— TUS PENSAMIENTOS ——

D A T E

A Book of Questions

WHAT WOULD YOU SAY TO THE PERSON
YOU LOST AND LATER FOUND?

¿QUE LE DIRIAS A LA PERSONA QUE PERDISTE Y
MAS TARDE ENCONTRASTE?

YOUR THOUGHTS

FECHA

THIS
LETTER
IS

A Book of Questions

DOODLE ALL YOU WANT

WHAT ARE THE THINGS THAT GIVE YOU PEACE OF MIND AND HELP RESTORE YOU?
¿QUE COSAS TE DAN SERENIDAD Y TE AYUDAN A SENTIRTE MEJOR?

——— TUS PENSAMIENTOS ———

DATE

A Book of Questions

>> A VAST CANVAS <<
WRITE, DRAW OR COLOR THIS SPACE

YOUR THOUGHTS

FECHA

THIS
LETTER
IS

DRAW YOUR OWN CONCLUSION

WHEN YOU WERE A CHILD AND PEERED INTO THE FUTURE, WHAT DID YOU THINK LIFE WOULD BE LIKE?

CUANDO ERAS CHICO Y PENSABAS EN EL FUTURO, ¿COMO CREIAS QUE SERIA LA VIDA?

———— TUS PENSAMIENTOS ————

DATE

A Book of Questions

TELL ME A SECRET,
A DREAM?
A NIGHTMARE?

¿PUEDES CONTARME UN SECRETO?
¿UN SUEÑO? ¿UNA PESADILLA?

———— YOUR THOUGHTS ————

THIS LETTER IS

FECHA

A Book of Questions

FACE THE DAY

WHAT KIND OF PERSON DO
YOU WANT TO BE?
¿QUE CLASE DE PERSONA DESEAS SER?

TUS PENSAMIENTOS

DATE

A Book of Questions

WRITE SOMETHING BEAUTIFUL TO THE WORLD.
(IT CAN BE IN YOUR SECRET LANGUAGE.)
¡ESCRÍBELE ALGO HERMOSO AL MUNDO!
(PUEDES ESCRIBIRLO EN TU IDIOMA SECRETO.)

─────── YOUR THOUGHTS ───────

THIS
LETTER
IS

FECHA

FACE YOURSELF TODAY

WHAT IS THE VERY WORST THING THAT CAN HAPPEN TO YOU?
¿QUE ES LO PEOR QUE TE PUEDE OCURRIR?

—— TUS PENSAMIENTOS ——

DATE

¿QUE COSAS AMAS?

— YOUR THOUGHTS —

♡ ———————————————————— ♡
♡ ———————————————————— ♡
♡ ———————————————————— ♡
♡ ———————————————————— ♡
♡ ———————————————————— ♡
♡ ———————————————————— ♡
♡ ———————————————————— ♡

FECHA

THIS
LETTER
IS

A Book of Questions

WHAT WOULD YOU DO WITH THE FREEDOM YOU ALWAYS WANTED? WHAT KIND OF PERSON WOULD YOU BE?

¿QUE HARIAS CON LA LIBERTAD QUE SIEMPRE HAS DESEADO? ¿QUE CLASE DE INDIVIDUO SERIAS?

DOODLE DOODLE DO

——— TUS PENSAMIENTOS ———

D A T E

A Book of Questions

WHAT ARE
¿CUALES SON

YOUR DEEPEST
TUS SUEÑOS

DREAMS?
DORADOS?

YOUR THOUGHTS

FECHA

THIS LETTER IS

A Book of Questions

IF YOU WERE TO **SHOCK** YOURSELF OUT OF YOUR SET WAYS, WHAT WOULD YOU DO?

SI PUDIERAS ZAFARTE DE TUS COSTUMBRES MAS ARRAIGADAS, ¿QUE HARIAS?

TUS PENSAMIENTOS

FACE FACTS

DATE

A Book of Questions

F YOU COULD BE AN ANIMAL, WHAT
WOULD YOU BE?
Si PUDIERAS SER UN ANIMAL¨ ¿CUAL SERIAS?

————— YOUR THOUGHTS —————

FECHA

F, LIKE ADAM, YOU COULD NAME A NEW
CREATURE, WHAT WOULD YOU CALL IT?
Si TU PUDIERAS, AL IGUAL QUE ADAN, DARLE EL NOMBRE
A UNA CRIATURA RECIEN CREADA, ¿QUE NOMBRE LE DARIAS?

————— YOUR THOUGHTS —————

FECHA

THIS
LETTER
IS

A Book of Questions

DRAW ON YOUR MEMORY

WHAT ARE THE THINGS THAT STRIKE YOU FUNNY?
¿QUE COSAS TE HACEN GRACIA?

TUS PENSAMIENTOS

DATE

A Book of Questions

>> CAVE PAINTING <<
WRITE · DRAW OR COLOR THIS SPACE

YOUR THOUGHTS

FECHA

THIS LETTER IS

A Book of Questions

FACE FORWARD

WHAT ARE THE GUIDING VALUES
OF YOUR LIFE?
¿QUE VALORES DIRIGEN TU VIDA?

———— TUS PENSAMIENTOS ————

D A T E

WHAT IS THE SPIRIT IN YOU THAT WILL BE
REMEMBERED WHEN YOU ARE GONE?
¿QUE LLEVAS EN EL ALMA QUE OTROS RECORDARAN
CUANDO YA TE HAYAS IDO?

———— TUS PENSAMIENTOS ————

D A T E

A Book of Questions

WHAT ARE YOU THANKFUL FOR ?
¿ DE QUE ESTAS AGRADECIDO ?
———— YOUR THOUGHTS ————

THIS
LETTER
IS

FECHA

A Book of Questions

DO A DOODLE ORTWOODLE

WHAT IS THE MOST WONDERFUL
IDEA YOU HAVE HAD
IN YOUR LIFE?

¿CUAL ES LA IDEA MAS MARAVILLOSA QUE
HAS TENIDO EN TODA TU VIDA?

—— TUS PENSAMIENTOS ——

DATE

A Book of Questions

IF YOU COULD BE A DIFFERENT ELEMENT...

EARTH — WATER — AIR OR FIRE

"WHICH WOULD YOU BE? WHY?"

SI PUDIERAS SER ALGUN ELEMENTO...
TIERRA, AGUA, AIRE O FUEGO... ¿CUAL SERIAS? ¿PORQUE?

——— YOUR THOUGHTS ———

FECHA

THIS LETTER IS

WHAT IS THE PRAYER YOU OFTEN SAY TO YOURSELF?
¿QUE ORACION REZAS A MENUDO?

TUS PENSAMIENTOS

LET'S FACE IT

D A T E

A Book of Questions

WHAT THINGS WOULD YOU DO TO CHANGE THE WORLD?

¿QUE COSAS HARIAS PARA CAMBIAR EL MUNDO?

— YOUR THOUGHTS —

FECHA

THIS LETTER IS

A Book of Questions

FACE VALUE

WHAT ARE YOUR OWN QUESTIONS?
(REMEMBER TO LISTEN TO YOUR
VOICE, DO NOT BE AFRAID.)
¿QUE PREGUNTAS TE HAS HECHO TU MISMO?
(RECUERDA, DEBES ESCUCHAR LA VOZ QUE
LLEVAS DENTRO DE TI. NO TENGAS
MIEDO.)

——— TUS PENSAMIENTOS ———

D A T E

A Book of Questions

— YOUR THOUGHTS —

THIS LETTER IS

FECHA

A Book of Questions

DRAWING ROOM

>> DO IT YOURSELF <<

———— TUS PENSAMIENTOS ————

D A T E

A Book of Questions

DOODLE ALL YOU WANT

>> DO IT YOURSELF <<

——— YOUR THOUGHTS ———

FECHA

A Book of Questions

>>DO IT YOURSELF<<

DRAW YOUR OWN CONCLUSION

————— TUS PENSAMIENTOS —————

D A T E

DON'T BE AFRAID TO ASK QUESTIONS.

Bill Zimmerman, the creator of *A Book of Questions*, has been a questioner all his life. A journalist for more than twenty years and a prize-winning editor, Zimmerman is special projects editor for *Newsday*, one of the nation's largest newspapers. His other books are *How to Tape Instant Oral Biographies*, a family oral history guide; *Make Beliefs*, a magical gift book for the imagination; *LifeLines: A Book of Hope*, which offers comforting thoughts to help us get through tough times in life; *The Little Book of Joy*, an interactive prayer book; *DOGMAS: Simple Truths from a Wise Pet*; *Make Beliefs for Kids*; and *A Book of Sunshine*, to move the clouds in your life. Zimmerman originally published *A Book of Questions* under the imprint of his kitchen-table press, Guarionex Press.

TOMBLOOM MAINTAINS THAT HE HAS ABOUT AN EQUAL NUMBER OF ANSWERS AS HE HAS QUESTIONS, AND THEY ARE FAIRLY EVENLY DISTRIBUTED AMONG THE DAILY AND MONTHLY PUBLICATIONS HE DRAWS FOR PERIODICALLY. AT HOME, HIS CHILDREN SEEM TO HAVE MANY MORE QUESTIONS THAN THERE ARE EVEN ANSWERS FOR. BUT THEN WE JUST KEEP ON DREAMING, DON'T WE?

Please Send Us Your Questions

Bill Zimmerman and Sourcebooks very much welcome your comments and suggestions as well as any questions that come from your own experiences and have helped you discover answers in your life.

If you do send your question, please consider giving us written permission (including your name and address) in case we want to add it to a future edition. For every suggestion or question we find useful, we will send you one of Zimmerman's books for free. A gift for a gift.

Please write to:

Bill Zimmerman
c/o Guarionex Press
201 West 77 Street
New York, NY 10024

Thank you.